SIL

TRADITIONAL BULGARIAN

COOKING

CONTENTS

Salads
Shopska Salad	5
Shepherd's Salad	5
Monk's Salad	6
Potato Salad	7
Russian Salad	8
Roasted Peppers Salad	8
Peppers and Eggplant Salad	9
Green Salad	10
Snezhanka Salad	10
White Salad	11
Beans Salad	12
Harvest Salad	13
Dobroudja Salad	13
Kyopoolou (Eggplant Dip)	14

Soups
Tarator	15
Shkembe Chorba	15
Bob Chorba (Beans Soup)	16
Bob Chorba (Monastery Style)	17
Meatball Soup	17
Zeleva Chorba (Cabbage Soup)	19
Spinach Soup	20
Vegetable Soup	20
Beef Soup	21
Lamb Soup	22
Milk Soup	23
Chicken Soup	23
Potato Soup	24
Fisherman Soup	25
Tomato Soup	27

Main Courses

With Meat
Kebapche	28
Kyufte	28
Shishche (Meat Skewer)	29
Moussaka	30

Sarmi
Lozovi Sarmi (Stuffed Grape Leaves)	31
Zelevi Sarmi (Stuffed Cabbage Leaves)	32
Stuffed Peppers	33
Meatballs In Rich Tomato Sauce	34
Monastery Gyuvetch	36
Kapama (Stewed Lamb with Onions)	37
Lamb with Scallions	38
Tas-Kebab (Lamb with Wine)	38
Drob Sarma (Lamb Liver with Rice)	39
Kavarma	40
Pork with Potatoes	41
Wine Kebab	42
Pork with Sauerkraut	43
Pork with Leeks	44
Pork with Rice	45
Pork Chops	46
Pork Stew	46
Gyuveche	47
Chomlek	48
Rabbit Chomlek	49
Stuffed Rabbit	50
Chicken Kavarma	51
Chicken Stew	52

Without Meat
Lentil Stew	53
Panagyurski Eggs	54
Mish-Mash (Eggs, Peppers, Chheese)	55
Cheese Stuffed Peppers	55
Cheese Shopski Style	56

Fried Courgettes	57
Potatoes au Gratin	58
Imambaialda (Stuffed Eggplants)	59
Eggplants in Tomato Sauce	60
Rice, Spinach and Mushrooms with Yoghurt	61
Tomato with Rice	62
Gyuvetch Without Meat	63
Peas with Potatoes	64

Pastries and Pies

Patatnik (Potato Dish)	64
Banitsa	66
Spinach Banitsa	66
Milk Banitsa	67
Phodopean Pie	68
Banitsa with Leeks and Cheese	69
Banitsa with Meat	70
Banitsa with Sauerkraut	71
Mekitsi (Fried Dough Pastry)	72
Baklava	73
Saraliiska Banitsa	74
Pumpkin Banitsa	74

SALADS

SHOPSKA SALAD

Ingredients:

4 ripe tomatoes
2 long cucumbers
1 onion, chopped
1 red or green pepper
1/3 bunch of parsley
2 tablespoons (olive) oil
3 tablespoons of red wine vinegar
1 cup Bulgarian cheese (or feta cheese)

How to prepare:

Chop all tomatoes (I recommend leaving the pieces bigger),the cucumbers and the pepper and put it in a bowl.

Add the onions and parsley. Sprinkle with the oil and vinegar and mix all together. Grate the feta on top.

SHEPHERD'S SALAD

Ingredients:

2 big tomatoes
1 cucumber
2 roasted peppers, peeled
1 bunch fresh green onions or 1 onion

1/3 lb marinated mushrooms
1/3 lb feta cheese
1/3 lb ham, chopped
1/3 lbs yellow cheese
4 hard-boiled eggs, chopped in four pieces
3 tablespoons vegetable oil
½ bunch fresh parsley
salt and vinegar to taste (I don't add vinegar)
olives to decorate

How to prepare:

Drain the mushrooms from the marinade; chop the parsley and the ham. Chop the vegetables and place in a mixing bowl, add the ham, parsley and mushrooms. Stir the mix and add salt and vinegar to taste. Pour the vegetable oil on top. Place in a serving platter and grate the feta and yellow cheese on top. Decorate with the eggs, olives and parsley.

Note: Don't give up if you don't have marinated mushrooms. You can make the salad without them – it is a real bliss anyway.

MONK'S SALAD

Ingredients:

2 large (2 lbs) eggplants
2 tomatoes, chopped
½ bunch mint
2 spring onion, chopped
2 tablespoons pomegranate molasses (see note)
2 tablespoons olive oil
hard-boiled eggs (optional)

How to prepare:

Using a fork, prick eggplants' skins all over, then place each one directly over a medium gas flame. Cook, turning every couple of minutes with thongs, for 12 minutes or until skin is charred and blackened and flesh is soft. You can cook the eggplants over a barbecue grill as well. Place the eggplants in a bowl and cool.

Peel the skin of the eggplants, then place flesh in a sieve over a bowl for a few seconds to drain. Using your hands, shred eggplants into strips. Arrange in a single layer in a large bowl with tomatoes, mint and spring onions.

Sprinkle the salad with pomegranate molasses and olive oil, season with salt and serve.

POTATO SALAD

Ingredients:

4 large potatoes, cut into cubes
a pinch of salt
crushed black pepper
2 onions (it is even better with scallions), finely chopped
the juice of half a lemon
2 tablespoons olive oil
some fresh parsley

How to prepare:

Peel and boil the potatoes for about 20 minutes, drain and leave to cool. In a salad bowl, add the onions, salt, pepper to taste, the lemon juice and olive oil. Cut the potatoes into cubes and add them in the salad bowl. Mix gently. Sprinkle with parsley before serving.

RUSSIAN SALAD

Ingredients:

1 lb potatoes
½ lb carrots
½ lb peas
½ lb pickled cucumbers, chopped
1 cup of mayonnaise
1 lb ham or salami, chopped

How to prepare:

Boil the potatoes, the carrots and the peas. Chop the potatoes and the carrots into small cubes. Mix all ingredients together and put the salad in the fridge for about an hour.

ROASTED PEPPERS SALAD

Ingredients:

6 peppers
2 large garlic cloves
3 teaspoons vegetable oil
1 ½ teaspoons vinegar
salt
fresh parsley, finely chopped
feta cheese (optional)

How to prepare:

Preheat oven to 400F.

Cut the tops of the peppers. Quarter the peppers lengthwise and discard the seeds and ribs.

Place the peppers, skin sides up, on a pan and bake until the skins are blistered and slightly blackened.

Transfer the peppers to a bowl, cover, and cool enough to touch.

Peel the skin and cut each pepper lengthwise in half.

Mince garlic.

Mix the peppers, garlic, oil and vinegar in a bowl and add salt to taste.

Cover the peppers, place in the fridge and allow to marinate (preferably overnight).

Sprinkle with parsley and serve.

Note: Before serving, you can sprinkle with crumbled cheese, if you like.

PEPPERS AND EGGPLANT SALAD

Ingredients:

1 eggplant
4 green peppers
2 tomatoes
½ cup walnuts, ground
½ cup vegetable oil
2 garlic cloves, crushed
some parsley
salt
vinegar

How to prepare:

Roast the eggplant and the peppers on a quick oven, grill, or open fire. Peel and cut in small pieces. Add the walnuts and garlic, and season with some of the oil, vinegar and salt. Mix well. Put the mixture in a serving dish and arrange on top the tomatoes, very thinly sliced. Sprinkle with parsley and pour on top the remaining oil.
Or you can arrange the salad as the one in the picture.

GREEN SALAD

Ingredients:

1 lettuce (your favourite type), finely chopped
1 cucumber, cut into two pieces by length, then sliced in discs
6 large radishes, cut into two and sliced
1 bunch scallions, finely chopped
½ bunch parsley, finely chopped
olive oil to taste
4-6 hard-boiled eggs
olives for decoration

How to prepare:

Mix all ingredients in a large bowl, add olive oil, salt and vinegar, mix well. You can put the eggs, chopped into very small pieces, in the salad or decorate with them if you cut them in two.

SNEZHANKA SALAD

Ingredients:

1 lb (4 cups) yoghurt
½ cucumber, peeled and chopped in cubes
1 garlic clove, finely chopped
a pinch of salt (don't add salt if you use pickled cucumbers)
1 tablespoon olive oil
a pinch of fresh dill, finely chopped

How to prepare:

Drain the cucumber as much as you can, strain the yoghurt, add all the ingredients together, refrigerate for at least an hour before serving. For best results, or if you don't have time to strain the yoghurt, add some sour cream to thicken the mixture.

Note: You can add ½ cup walnuts, very finely ground, on top.

WHITE SALAD

Ingredients:

2-3 cucumbers
2 cups cottage cheese
1 cup cream
½ cup walnuts
2-3 garlic cloves
dill, finely chopped
sunflower oil
salt

3 eggs (optional)

How to prepare:

Peel and dice the cucumbers, add the cottage cheese, cream, walnuts and garlic, the oil, dill and salt to taste.

Beat the mixture, pour into a plate and garnish (optional) with hard boiled eggs, cut in two.

BEANS SALAD

Ingredients:

½ lb beans of choice (I prefer butter or haricot beans)
1 large red onion, chopped
4-5 tablespoons vinegar
6 tablespoons olive oil (you can use sunflower oil too)
½ teaspoon ground black pepper
salt to taste
parsley
olives

How to prepare:

Soak the beans in water overnight. Drain the water, add fresh water and boil until the beans soften. Leave to cool. Discard the water.

Mix the beans and the onions. Season with vinegar, olive oil, black pepper, salt and parsley. Garnish with olives and serve.

HARVEST SALAD

Ingredients:

½ cup chopped walnuts
1 bunch spinach, rinsed and torn into bite-size pieces
½ cup dried cranberries
½ cup crumbled blue cheese
2 tomatoes, chopped
1 avocado, peeled, pitted and diced
½ red onion, thinly sliced
2 tablespoons red raspberry jam (with seeds)
2 tablespoons red wine vinegar
1/3 cup walnut or olive oil
freshly ground black pepper to taste
salt to taste

How to prepare:

Preheat oven to 375F. Arrange walnuts in a single layer on a baking sheet. Toast in the oven for 5 minutes or until nuts begin to brown.

In a large bowl, mix the spinach, walnuts, cranberries, blue cheese, tomatoes, avocado and red onion.

In a small bowl, whisk together jam, vinegar, walnut oil, pepper and salt. Pour over the salad just before serving.

DOBROUDJA SALAD

Ingredients:

½ lb cooked rice
2 large carrots, chopped in strips
1 large cucumber
dill, finely chopped
salt to taste
vinegar to taste
vegetable oil to taste
olives, cut in two

How to prepare:

Mix all the ingredients. Season with salt, vinegar and oil.

KYOPOOLOU (EGGPLANT DIP)

Ingredients:

2 big eggplants, chopped
4 red or green peppers (or both), chopped
3 medium tomatoes, peeled &chopped
3 cloves of garlic, crushed
a bunch of fresh parsley, finely chopped
1 cup vinegar
½ cup sunflower or olive oil
1 tablespoon salt

How to prepare:

Roast the eggplants and the peppers in the oven, peel their skin and cut into small pieces. Add the tomatoes and the garlic. Add the oil and vinegar, salt to taste, mix well. Sprinkle with parsley before serving.

SOUPS

TARATOR

Ingredients:

1 long cucumber, chopped or grated (I prefer it peeled)
1 garlic clove, minced or smashed
4 cups yoghurt
1 cup water
1 teaspoon salt (my family likes it saltier)
1 tablespoon dill, finely chopped
4 big pecans, well crushed
3 teaspoons olive oil

How to prepare:

Put all those together. When ready, garnish with olive oil (or other favourite oil). Best when chilled.

SHKEMBE CHORBA

Ingredients:

1 lb tripe (calf belly)
1 cup (sunflower) oil
2 cups fresh milk
1 teaspoon paprika
1 tablespoon ground black pepper
1 tablespoon salt

2 garlic cloves, peeled and thinly diced
1/3 cup red wine vinegar
dried hot chili pepper mix

How to prepare:

Boil the tripe for about 30 minutes, add oil, milk, black pepper and paprika and boil for another 30 minutes, occasionally topping up the water. The more you cook it, the better it will taste.

Mix some salt, garlic and vinegar in a separate cup, let it soak fir about an hour.

Serve hot, garnish with the garlic and vinegar mixture and the hot chili peppers.

BOB CHORBA (BEANS SOUP)

Ingredients:
1 lb beans (use white, if possible: haricot, fava, etc.)
2 qt. water
2 onions, chopped
2 tablespoons sunflower oil
3 tablespoons flour
1 tablespoon paprika
4 tomatoes (or a can of tomatoes)
1 tablespoon oregano (or dried mint)
salt to taste

How to prepare:

Soak the beans into the water overnight. On the next morning, drain off the water, add the same amount and bring to boil. If you don't want to wait a day, you can simply boil the beans for an hour, then discard the water, add water again and bring to boil again. Simmer gently for an hour or until the beans soften. In a separate pan, fry the onions in the oil until golden brown, add the flour, stir and fry for less than a minute. Add the paprika, stir and add to the beans. Add the tomatoes and oregano as well. Leave the soup to simmer on low heat for about 20 minutes or until the beans is fully cooked.

BOB CHORBA (MONASTERY STYLE)

Ingredients:

1lb white beans
2 carrots, finely chopped
½ celery stalk
1 onion
2 tomatoes, grated
2 peppers, sliced
1 chili pepper (optional)
a pinch of parsley, finely chopped
a pinch of mint or oregano
2 tablespoons sunflower oil
salt to taste

How to prepare:

Soak the beans in cold water, drain and pour fresh water. Boil in a pot together with oil, carrots, onion and celery. Boil until beans are soft, then add the peppers, tomatoes and mint. Add salt to taste and boil for another 15 – 20 minutes. Sprinkle with parsley and serve.

MEATBALL SOUP

Ingredients:

1 lb ground meat (we prefer 60% pork and 40 % beef)
6 tablespoons rice
1 teaspoon paprika
1 teaspoon dried savory
salt & pepper to taste
2 tablespoons flour
6 cups water
2 beef bouillon cubes
½ bunch scallions, chopped
1 green bell pepper, chopped
2 medium carrots, peeled & thinly sliced
3 tomatoes, peeled & chopped
½ bunch parsley, minced
1 egg
lemon juice

How to prepare:

Mix the ground meat, rice, paprika and savory. Season to taste with salt and pepper and mix well. Form into small balls, then roll in flour.

Mix water, bouillon cubes, 1 tablespoon salt, 1 teaspoon pepper, scallions, the bell pepper, carrots and tomatoes in a large pot. Cover, bring to boil, reduce heat and simmer for 30 minutes.

Add the meatballs, cover and bring to boil again. Reduce heat and simmer for 30 minutes or until the meat and rice are cooked.

Add parsley 5 minutes before taking the dish off the heat. Taste and add more salt and pepper if needed.

Just before serving, beat an egg with some lemon juice and add to the soup.

ZELEVA CHORBA (CABBAGE SOUP)

It is extremely healthy and nutritious. It is also used in healthy diets.

Ingredients:

1 medium cabbage head, chopped
6 medium carrots, chopped
1 small celery root with stalks and leaves, chopped& peeled
6 clove of garlic, minced
3 onions, chopped
6 sweet red or green peppers, chopped and seeded
1 lb tomatoes
a pinch of salt
1 teaspoon sugar
2 tablespoons sunflower oil
1/3 cup crumbs
4 vegetable bouillon cubes

How to prepare:

Cover the whole tomatoes with water and boil just until the skins begin to split. Remove from the heat, set aside and allow cooling.

Chop the carrots into small pieces and put into a large pot with about a litter of water and boil for 10 minutes. Remove from the heat and add garlic, onions, peppers, celery and cabbage.

Slip off the skins of the tomatoes, chop and add into the pot. Add the oil, the crumbs, the cubes of bouillon and enough water to cover all the vegetables. Simmer for a couple of hours or until vegetables are fully cooked.

SPINACH SOUP

Ingredients:

½ bunch of spinach leaves, chopped
2 tablespoons butter
2 tablespoons flour
2 l water
½ gallon milk
ground black pepper
salt to taste
cheese
croutons

How to prepare:

Boil the spinach in the salted water, then drain it and make it into puree.

Heat up the butter and add the flour, cook until brown, add to the spinach puree. Dilute with milk and half of the water in which you had boiled the spinach. Add the pepper and boil for another 5 – 10 minutes.

Serve with croutons and pieces of cheese.

Note: Following the same recipe, you can prepare nettle soup.

VEGETABLE SOUP

Ingredients:

2 potatoes, diced
2 carrots, diced
½ celery, diced
2 peppers, sliced
¼ of a medium sized cabbage, finely chopped
1 onion, finely chopped
3 tomatoes, diced
1 beetroot, diced
1 tablespoon flour
1 teaspoon paprika
4 tablespoons yoghurt
1 egg
1 cup grated cheese, mozzarella works best
2 tablespoons sunflower oil
salt to taste
a pinch of parsley, finely chopped

How to prepare:

Put the celery, cabbage, peppers, carrots and salt in the water and boil. When soft, add the potatoes.

Boil the beetroot separately.

Stew the onion until soft; then add the flour, paprika and the tomatoes. Add the mixture to the boiling vegetables and boil for another half an hour. Add the beetroot at the end. Thicken with an egg beaten in yoghurt. Sprinkle with parsley and grated cheese and serve.

BEEF SOUP

Ingredients:

1 lb beef shin, cut into large pieces
½ lb carrots, cut into large pieces
1 onion, quartered
3-4 medium-sized potatoes, halved
1 stick of celery, chopped
2 bay leaves
1 teaspoon salt
1/8 teaspoon pepper
2 cloves of garlic
some fresh flat leave parsley, chopped

How to prepare:

In a frying pan, brown beef, drain and transfer to a large saucepan with water. Add bay leaves and cloves of garlic, season with salt and pepper and cook for 3 hours on low heat. Add the carrots, celery and potatoes. Cook for another 50-60 minutes. Sprinkle with fresh parsley and serve.

LAMB SOUP

1 lb lamb
a bunch of green onion, finely chopped
1/6 lb rice
1 green pepper, finely chopped
3 tomatoes, grated
1 egg
pepper (corns)
a bunch of parsley
hogweed
salt
the juice of half a lemon

How to prepare:

Boil the meat together with few corn peppers for about 30 minutes. Add the onion and the pepper and boil for another 10 minutes. Add the rice, stirring, and boil for another 15 minutes. Add the hogweed and the tomatoes. When the meat is cooked, remove the bones and cut in big pieces. Add it back into the water.

Beat the egg, add the lemon juice and add the mixture to the soup. Serve hot.

MILK SOUP

Ingredients:

300 ml milk
1/6 lb butter
2 eggs
¼ lb feta cheese, crushed
½ cup rice
savory or pepper
salt

How to prepare:

Boil the milk and add 3 cups of warm water. Add the rice and salt. Boil until the rice is cooked.

Take off the heat, season, mix in the butter and thicken with beaten eggs.

Add the cheese and serve.

Note: You can add croutons if you like.

CHICKEN SOUP

Ingredients:

1 large chicken
1 large stalk celery, finely chopped
2 tomatoes, diced and seeded
1 cup parsley, chopped
2 eggs
1 onion, diced
2 carrots, cubed
1 red pepper, diced
2 cups fine egg noodles (vermicelli)
lemon juice, salt and pepper to taste

How to prepare:

Thoroughly clean the chicken and wash (skinned, fat and loose skin at the neck and rump removed).

Place in a saucepan with salted water, cover and bring to boil. When tender, remove and set aside. Sieve bouillon and return to saucepan.

Add onions and cook for 5 minutes.

Add carrots and cook for 10 minutes.

Add celery and red pepper and cook for 5 minutes.

Add noodles, parsley and tomatoes and cook for 15 minutes.

In the meantime, remove legs and wings and use for cold meat. Be sure all bones are removed. Chop the remaining chicken meat and add to the soup. Simmer for 10 minutes and cool.

Beat the eggs. Add the lemon juice. Very slowly, add to the soup, stirring gently but constantly.

POTATO SOUP

Ingredients:

2 lbs potatoes, cubed
4 spring onions or 1 large onion, chopped
3 eggs
3 carrots, chopped
2 tomatoes, peeled and chopped or 2 tablespoons tomato paste
vermicelli to taste, depends how thick you like it
a handful of savory or oregano
salt to taste
1 teaspoon paprika
3 tablespoons vegetable oil
3 chicken bouillon cubes
the juice of half to 1 lemon, to taste
parsley

How to prepare:

In a large saucepan, fry the onions and the carrots in the oil. When soft, add the paprika and stir. Immediately pour water in the saucepan, a little at first, stirring. Then pour 1.5 l to 2 l water.

Add the potatoes and savory the bouillon cubes and boil until the potatoes are cooked. Add vermicelli and tomatoes and boil until vermicelli is cooked.

In a bowl, whisk the eggs and add the lemon juice.

When the soup is ready, take it off the heat and cool.

Add the eggs, stirring.

Serve hot.

Note: You can sprinkle the soup with ground black pepper before serving if you like.

FISHERMAN SOUP (MONASTERY STYLE)

Ingredients:

1 lb fish (Bulgarians prefer carp), chopped and salted
50 ml sunflower oil
3-4 spring onions or 1 onion, chopped
¼ lb tomatoes, peeled and chopped
1/6 lb peppers (one or two), chopped
1-2 carrots, chopped
2 hot chili peppers (optional)
1/3 lb potatoes, cubed
1-2 handfuls rice
4 olives
1 teaspoon thyme
1 tablespoon parsley, finely chopped
ground black pepper to taste
1 lemon
salt to taste

How to prepare:

Pour 1 – 1.5 l water in a big saucepan and bring to boil. Add onion, carrots, peppers, hot chili peppers, tomatoes, potatoes, thyme, oil and salt.

When potatoes and carrots are soft, add fish and rice. After 15-20 minutes add olives.

When the fish and rice are cooked, take the soup off the heat.

Serve hot, sprinkled with parsley and ground black pepper, garnished with a slice of lemon.

TOMATO SOUP

Ingredients:

2 tablespoons olive oil
1 tablespoon butter
1 large white onion, finely chopped
1 large clove garlic, peeled and smashed
2 tablespoons all-purpose flour
3 cups chicken broth
28-oz. can whole peeled tomatoes, pureed
1 ½ teaspoons sugar
1 sprig fresh thyme
salt to taste
ground black pepper to taste
3 tablespoons sliced fresh basil
parsley, finely chopped

How to prepare:

In a saucepan, heat the oil and butter over medium-low heat until the butter melts. Add the onion and garlic and cook, stirring occasionally, until soft but not browned (about 8 minutes). Add the flour and stir to coat the onion and garlic.

Add the broth, tomatoes, sugar, thyme and ¼ teaspoon each salt and pepper. Bring to a simmer over medium-high heat while stirring the mixture to make sure that the flour is not sticking to the bottom of the saucepan. Reduce the heat to low, cover and simmer for 40 minutes.

Discard the thyme sprig. Season to taste with salt and pepper.

Serve warm but not hot, sprinkled with parsley.

MAIN COURSES

WITH MEAT

KEBAPCHE

A meatball made of minced meat and spices and shaped like a sausage. Same as the *kyufte* but does not contain onions. It has to be grilled otherwise you will get something different which probably won't be called *kebapche* (for comparison *kyufte* can also be fried.) Eat it with *Shopska salad* and French fries with feta cheese. Delicious.

Ingredients:

2 lbs mince meat (60% pork, 40% beef)
1 tablespoon salt
1 tablespoon ground black pepper
½ teaspoon cumin
1 clove of garlic, minced (my family prefers it with garlic but it is not necessary)

How to prepare:

Mix all ingredients together, mix well. Leave in the fridge for at least 30 minutes. Take out and roll in sausage like pieces. Make about 30 pieces.

KYUFTE

Again, a meatball made of minced meat and spices shaped like a meatball slapped with a spatula. Same as *kebapche* but contains chopped onions too. You can grill, fry or bake it. As with *kebapche,* eat it with *Shopska salad* and French fries with feta cheese.

Ingredients:

2 lbs mince meat (60% pork, 40% beef)
1 onion, chopped
1 tablespoon salt
1 tablespoon ground black pepper
1 teaspoon cumin
1 clove of garlic, minced (my family prefers it with garlic but it is not necessary)

How to prepare:

Mix all ingredients together, mix well Leave in the fridge for at least 30 minutes. Take out and shape in balls, then flatten in patty-like pieces.

Make about 20 pieces.

Note: If you are going to fry the meatballs, add an egg in the mixture.

If you think this recipe is exactly like the one for *kebapche,* look again – this one has onion on it and it makes all the difference.

SHISHCHE (SHASHLIK, MEAT SKEWER)

Ingredients:

2 lbs pork shoulder, cut into big cubes
100 ml vodka
1 tablespoon honey
1 tablespoon black pepper

1 tablespoon mustard
discs of onion
red or green peppers, chopped
bacon
tomatoes (optional)
mushrooms (optional)

How to prepare:

The secret of the *shishche* is that the meat should soak in marinade.

The marinade: mix the honey, mustard, vodka, salt and pepper, Soak the meat pieces into it and leave the bowl in the refrigerator.

Use a skewer to arrange alternating pieces meat, onion, pepper, bacon, mushrooms, tomatoes, then again. Grill on a barbecue until the meat is done to your liking.

MOUSSAKA

One of the several Bulgarian foods confused in the West for being Greek. Make the dish and you will not want to leave the table until you have finished up the entire baking pan. Eat this with some yoghurt on top.

Moussaka is rather famous on the Balkans and in the Middle East. Its recipe is different depending on the region, but in general it is based either on potatoes (Bulgaria) or eggplant (Greece) and the top layer is often custard. Grated cheese or bread crumbs are also often sprinkled on top.

Ingredients:

2 lbs potatoes, peeled and cut in small cubes

1 lb ground meat (we prefer to mix 60% pork, 40% beef)
2 onions, finely chopped
4 eggs
2 cups milk
2 tablespoons paprika
1 tablespoon salt
1 teaspoon crushed black pepper
½ cup olive oil

How to prepare:

Cook the onion in ¼ cup oil in a pan until golden brown. Add the meat, half of the salt, the pepper and the paprika. Fry until the meat gets brown. Remove the pan from the heat.

Add the potatoes, add the rest of the salt and mix well.

In casserole pan, put the rest of the oil and add the mixture. Cook about 40 minutes on 425 F.

Mix the eggs and the milk separately and pour on top. Cook for another 10 minutes or until the top turns brownish.

SARMI

Another Bulgarian dish confused with its Greek cousin. *Sarmi* are made of grape or cabbage leaves stuffed with combination of rice and mince meat and then boiled. They can be served both hot or cold to your liking.

LOZOVI SARMI (STUFFED GRAPE LEAVES)

Definitely try them with some yoghurt on top.

Ingredients:

15-20 grape leaves
3 onions, chopped
2 cups white rice
1 teaspoon dried celery or oregano
3 tablespoons oil
1 teaspoon paprika
3 cups water

How to prepare:

Steam the grape leaves. Fry the onion in the oil until brown, add the rice, paprika, celery and oregano and add the water. Boil until the water is absorbed. Use the mixture to fill the leaves, shaping them like small bundles. Put in a pot, fill with water so the bundles are fully submerged, and boil for about 45 minutes on 350 F. You can bake them in the oven in a baking dish full of water instead.

Note: *Sarmi* can be prepared without meat if you are a vegetarian.

ZELEVI SARMI

Ingredients:

1 cabbage, pickled
3 onions, chopped
1 carrot
1 root celery
2 cups white rice
1 teaspoon salt
1 teaspoon ground black pepper

a bunch of parsley, chopped

How to prepare:

De-leaf the cabbage. Mix the onion, carrot and the celery and cook in the oil until the onion turns golden. Add the rice, parsley, salt and the pepper.

Use the mixture to fill the leaves, shaping them as small bundles. The best way to do it is to put some mixture on a big leaf, put a small leaf on top and wrap the big leaf around the small one. Put in a pot, cover with water and boil. You can bake them in the oven in a casserole pan full of water instead.

Note: *Sarmi* can be served with tomato sauce as well as with béchamel sauce. Try!

STUFFED PEPPERS

Very, very delicious meal. It is pretty much what it says: green or red peppers stuffed with ground beef or pork and rice and boiled. Sometimes the peppers are topped with a seasoned tomato sauce or whisked eggs. As *sarmi,* can be served with tomato sauce or béchamel sauce.

Ingredients:

6 green or red peppers
½ lb minced meat (we prefer 60% pork and 40% beef)
1 cup white rice
2 tablespoons vegetable oil
1 tomato, peeled and minced
1 carrot, minced
1 onion, minced

1 teaspoon paprika
1 clove of garlic, minced
1 tablespoon parsley, minced
a pinch of oregano, cumin, savory, black pepper

How to prepare:

Fry the onion in the oil until turns golden; add the garlic, carrot, red pepper, oregano, cumin, savory, black pepper and the meat.

In a separate pan, cook the rice in some oil for about 5 minutes and then add a cup of water. Let it simmer until the rice absorbs it all. When ready, add everything together.

Add the tomato and stir well until well mixed. Take off the heat and use the mixture to stuff the peppers. Put the stuffed peppers in a casserole or a pot, fill with water just below the top of the peppers and bake/cook for about 30 minutes on 400 F.

Note: Stuffed peppers can be prepared without meat if you are a vegetarian.

MEATBALLS IN RICH TOMATO SAUCE

Ingredients:
For the meatballs:
1 ½ lb mince meat (we prefer 60 % pork and 40 % beef)
1 medium onion, finely chopped
1 egg
fresh parsley leaves, finely chopped
2 teaspoons savory
1 teaspoon cumin
salt

freshly ground black pepper
2-3 tablespoons flour
For the sauce:
3 tablespoons sunflower oil
1 onion, finely chopped
1 clove of garlic
2 big tomatoes, peeled and diced
1 small celeriac, peeled and diced
2 teaspoons paprika
1 tablespoon fresh parsley leaves, finely chopped
1 tablespoon fresh celery leaves, finely chopped
½ cube vegetable bouillon
Optional:
2 potatoes, diced
1 green sweet pepper, diced

How to prepare:

First, prepare the meatballs: mix the meat, onion, the egg and all the spices. Mix well and, with wet hands, form balls (with the size of a ping-pong ball). Roll them in flour, so they are thoroughly covered. If the mince meat mix is too sticky, you can add some bread crumbs – for this quantity, a slice of bread will be enough.

In a big saucepan, heat the oil. Add onion and garlic and fry them for about 2 minutes. Add the green pepper, stir and fry for another 2-3 minutes. Take off the heat, add paprika and stir well.

Pour in the hot bouillon, add celeriac and potatoes and boil again.

In another saucepan, heat salted water. When hot, add the meatballs and boil for just 5 minutes. Take the meatballs out with a slotted spoon.

When the potatoes are cooked, add the meatballs and tomatoes and cook for 15 minutes or until the meatballs are cooked.

Add fresh herbs, cook for another 5 minutes. Serve warm.

MONASTERY GYUVETCH

This dish used to be prepared at *The Rilla Monastery* kitchen. *The Rilla Monastery* is one of the most famous Bulgarian tourist attractions and a milestone in Bulgarian culture and religion – it has survived almost untouched through the years of Ottoman yoke and has provided a shelter and education to many people in the years of oppression.

Ingredients:

2 lbs beef
4 tomatoes, chopped
½ lb mushrooms
1 cup rice
1 onion, chopped
15 olives
a bunch of parsley
2 tablespoons vegetable oil
1 tablespoon butter
1 tablespoon sugar
2 ½ cups beef bouillon
black pepper, paprika and salt

How to prepare:

Cut the beef into cubes or small pieces and fry in a pan with a little oil for about 5 minutes or until brown. Add the onions, beef bouillon and paprika. 5 minutes later, add the mushrooms and rice. Simmer for about 15 minutes. Add the tomatoes, salt to taste, butter, sugar and olives. Cook for another 5 minutes.

Preheat oven to 400F. Transfer the content of the pan into a baking dish and cook for about 30 minutes.

Sprinkle with parsley and black pepper and serve.

KAPAMA (STEWED LAMB WIT ONIONS)

Ingredients:

1 lb lamb meat, chopped in cubes
water
2 tablespoons vinegar
½ cup wine
3 tablespoons flour to cover the meat with
ground black pepper to taste
1 tablespoon tomato paste
a pinch of cinnamon
2 cloves of garlic, chopped
parsley, finely chopped
a pinch of mint or oregano
bay or laurel leaves

How to prepare:

Prepare marinade of the water, vinegar, wine, pepper, mint, parsley, bay leaves and steep the meat in it for about 2 hours. You can cut it in pieces before or after steeping it. Roll the bits of meat in the flour and fry them in the hot oil. Add salt, pepper, the tomato paste, cinnamon and garlic. Add also 2 glasses of water and let the meat stew until the sauce is thickened.

Serve with a potato salad. Sprinkle the meat with parsley immediately before serving.

LAMB WITH SCALLIONS

Ingredients:

2 lbs lamb meat, cut into pieces
5 bunches of scallions, chopped
hot water
1 teaspoon salt
1 teaspoon paprika
1 teaspoon black pepper, ground
2 tablespoons butter

How to prepare:

Put the meat into wide baking dish. Add ½ cup hot water and the butter and put in the oven for about 2 hours at 300F. After the first half an hour, add the onions, salt, paprika, black pepper and 1 ½ cup hot water, stir and continue cooking. In another 30 minutes, add ½ cup hot water and stir. Add ½ cup hot water in every 30 minutes within the 2 hours of cooking. After the two hours, cover with a baking sheet and cook for additional ½ hour (2 ½ hours total cooking time). Sprinkle with parsley and serve warm.

TAS – KEBAB (LAMB WITH WINE)

Ingredients:

2 lbs lamb roast, cubed
2 medium onions, chopped

1 tablespoon pepper
6 large juniper berries
1 medium bay leaf
1 can tomato paste
2 tablespoons butter
¼ cup white wine
2 cups beef broth

How to prepare:

Mix the meat, onions, pepper, juniper, bay leaf and tomato paste. Marinate for 2 hours.
Remove bay leaf and juniper.
Sauté the meat and onions in butter for 10 minutes or until golden.
Add wine and simmer until it evaporates.
Add broth and simmer for 50 minutes. Serve with rice or pasta.

DROB SARMA (LAMB LIVER WITH RICE)

Ingredients:

2 lbs lamb liver, hearts and kidneys, cut into cubes
2 eggs
½ cup rice
2 bunches of scallions, finely chopped
1 cup yoghurt
mint
pepper
½ cup butter
salt to taste

How to prepare:

Boil the liver, hearts and kidneys in salted water about 30 minutes.

Cook the scallions in the butter and some water for about 5 minutes, add the rice, liver, hearts and kidneys, pepper and mint and cook for 5 minutes more. Add 2 cups of the lamb bouillon and boil for 20 minutes.

Put the rice mixture and the meat in a cooking pan, put in the oven and bake for 30 minutes at 375F.

Beat the eggs with the yoghurt, pour over the lamb and rice and bake for another 10 minutes.

KAVARMA

This is one of the most popular meals in Bulgaria. However, it is not so famous outside the country. The ingredients and How to prepares depend on the region. Almost every part of Bulgaria has its own *Kavarma* recipe. In general, the meal consists of marinated cooked meat and vegetables. It could be mild or spicy depending on the region and the likings. Goes perfectly well with beer or wine.

Ingredients:

2 lbs pork meat, cut into cubes
½ cup oil
2 big leaks
1 tablespoon tomato sauce or puree
1 tablespoon paprika
a pinch of crushed black pepper
1 cup red or white wine
1 onion, chopped
2 carrots

2 bay leaves
a pinch of parsley
1 hot pepper (you can also prepare the dish without it if you like)

How to prepare:

Mix wine, tomato sauce, paprika and black pepper to make the marinade.

Add the cut disks carrots to the pork and cook in very hot oil until meat starts to brown. Take out and soak into marinade for about 30 minutes.

Use the same hot oil to cook the leaks, cut in disks, add ½ cup water to it and cook until soft (about 5 minutes). Add the meat and the remaining marinade to the leaks; reduce the heat and simmer until most of the water is gone. Add the bailey leaves, chopped onion and the hot pepper and cook for about 5 more minutes.

Sprinkle with parsley and serve. Goes well with French fries or white rice.

PORK WITH POTATOES

The recipe works with any meat as well as with pork. Give it a try!

Ingredients:

1.5 lb pork meat, cut into cubes
1 onion, chopped
1 carrot, chopped
a stick of celery, sliced
1 Italian pepper, sliced
1 teaspoon paprika

1 teaspoon salt
5 potatoes, cut into cubes
1 can (6-8 oz.) tomato sauce
2 tablespoons parsley
2 cups hot water
¼ cup vegetable oil

How to prepare:

Put the meat in a pan, add the salt and the oil, cover and cook at medium heat for about 15 minutes, stirring occasionally. Add the carrot and the onion and stir. In about 5 minutes, add the celery and the green pepper and stir. Stirring is important. Add a little water – to cover the bottom - cover and cook for 30 minutes. Add the potatoes and cook for another 15 minutes or until the potatoes are soft. Add the tomato sauce, parsley and stir. Cook for another 5 minutes, then turn off the heat and let the pan stay on it for another 10 minutes. Sprinkle with parsley and serve.

Note: If you cook chicken, reduce cooking time to 10 minutes instead of ½ hour.

WINE KEBAB

Ingredients:

1 lb pork, cut into cubes
4 onions, chopped
1 cup wine, preferably red
½ cup hot water
1 bay leaf
ground black pepper
½ cup oil

salt

How to prepare:

Fry the meat and the onions in the oil, after they are golden, add salt and ground black pepper and mix well. Add ½ cup hot water and 1 cup red wine and simmer for about an hour or until the meat is fully cooked. Add water, if necessary.

Note: Kebab is usually served with potato puree or white rice as in the picture.

PORK WITH SAUERKRAUT

Ingredients:

1 ½ lbs pork, chopped
4 tablespoons vegetable oil
150-200 ml hot water
3 lbs sauerkraut, finely chopped
1-2 onions, chopped
1 teaspoon paprika
4-5 hot chili peppers (optional)
ground black pepper

How to prepare:

In a deep pan or saucepan, fry the meat in ½ oil and a little water for 10-15 minutes maximum, then take out.

Fry the onion in the same oil. Add the paprika, stir and add the water.

Add the pork meat. Simmer on mild heat for 20-30 minutes.

In a baking dish, pour the rest ½ of the oil and add the sauerkraut.

Preheat oven to 375F. Put the baking dish in the oven. Stew the cabbage for 20-30 minutes or until soft.

Add the meat and the hot chili peppers. Put the baking dish in the oven again.

Bake until ready.

Sprinkle with ground black pepper and serve hot.

PORK WITH LEEKS

Ingredients:

2 lbs pork, chopped into bites
6 sticks of leeks, chopped
2 tablespoons tomato puree
1 coffee cup red wine
vegetable oil
salt to taste
1 teaspoon sugar
ground black pepper to taste
1 teaspoon paprika
1 tablespoon savory
parsley to taste

How to prepare:

In a deep pan or saucepan, fry the meat in the oil for 10-15 minutes or until soft. Take it out and put in a plate.

Fry the leeks in the same oil. Add the tomato puree, all the spices, some water and the wine. Add the meat.

Simmer on low heat until the water and wine evaporate. If the meat is not fully cooked, add a little water again and simmer until evaporates. If necessary, repeat until the meat is fully cooked.

Sprinkle with parsley and serve warm.

PORK WITH RICE

Ingredients:

2 lbs pork (lean, if possible), chopped in bites
1 ½ cup rice
1 large onion, finely chopped
1 large carrot, finely chopped
sunflower oil to your taste but not more than 4 tablespoons
½ teaspoon ground black pepper
½ teaspoon paprika
salt to taste
hot water

How to prepare:

In a deep pan, fry the meat in the half of the oil for 10-15 minutes. If necessary, add ½ coffee cup hot water and add black pepper, salt and paprika. Cook until the meat is slightly soft.

In another pan or saucepan, fry the onion in the other half of the oil. When soft, add the rice and fry for some minutes, stirring all the time. Transfer the ingredients in an oiled baking dish.

Add the meat, add 5 cups hot water and cook at 375F until the rice absorbs the water.

PORK CHOPS

This is a general recipe from Bulgaria. Feel free to add spices to taste and substitute the white wine for red.

Ingredients:

4 pork chops
2 medium carrots, finely chopped
salt and black pepper
1 large onion, chopped
½ glass white wine
3 garlic cloves, finely chopped
4 large mushrooms, chopped
½ lb tomatoes, chopped
2 celery sticks, finely chopped

How to prepare:

Season the chops with salt and pepper and fry in a frying pan until brown. When ready, take them out.
In the same pan, cook the rest of the ingredients for 5-10 minutes.
Preheat the oven to 440F.
Put the chops in an oven dish, cover with the vegetable mixture and cook for about 20 minutes.
Serve with boiled or mashed potatoes.

PORK STEW

Ingredients:

2 ½ lbs pork, chopped
4 tablespoons vegetable oil

2 lbs onion, finely chopped
1 teaspoon flour
2 tablespoons tomato paste
1 lb tomatoes, fresh or canned, finely chopped if fresh
1 teaspoon paprika
savory to taste
½ cup red wine
a little butter
2 bay leaves
parsley
ground black pepper to taste
salt to taste

How to prepare:

In a saucepan, fry the meat in the oil for 10-15 minutes, then take it out.

In the same oil, fry the onion until soft. Add the tomato paste, paprika and a little water. Add the meat. Add the wine, a little warm water, savory, bay leaves and black pepper.

Simmer until almost ready. Add the tomatoes and flour, stirring constantly.

Simmer until the meat is fully cooked. Add the butter, sprinkle with parsley and serve.

GYUVECHE

Gyuveche is a popular catch-all dish you can make it with just about anything you have in the fridge. It has gotten its name from the pottery in which it is cooked (in the picture).

Ingredients:

½ lb feta cheese (or any other kind but feta works best)
1 egg
½ onion, chopped
tomato paste
parsley or dill, chopped
any kind of cooked meat (pork, chicken or beef) or sausages you have
vegetables: peppers, small hot pepper, mushrooms, cooked potatoes (optional)

How to prepare:

Put the onions and the tomato paste to cover the bottom.
Chop or dice all ingredients you have gathered. Make alternating layers of cheese, meat and vegetables but make sure you have cheese on top. Bake in the oven at 375F for 20 minutes or until the cheese is melted. Break the egg on top and put back in the oven for another 5-10 minutes.

CHOMLEK

Ingredients:

4 lbs veal knuckle
2 lbs potatoes, peeled and chopped
6 onions, chopped
500 ml red wine
15 garlic cloves
2 hot peppers

1 tablespoon paprika
pepper (corns)
3 bay leaves

How to prepare:

Cut the knuckle in big pieces. Put all ingredients in a clay pot, cover and cook at 375F for about 5 hours. Serve hot.

RABBIT CHOMLEK

Ingredients:

1 rabbit, chopped as in the picture
5 onions, chopped
½ lb pickling onions
5-6 cloves of garlic, chopped
1 cup white wine
1 tablespoon vinegar
3 bay leaves
10 peppercorns
3 whole allspice berries
1 tablespoon paprika
1 teaspoon sugar
5 tablespoons vegetable oil
salt to taste

How to prepare:

Put the rabbit in a large earthen pot. Add (arrange around the rabbit, if possible) the onion, pickling onions, and garlic. Add the vinegar and wine. Cover (barely) with water.

Add the bay leaves, black pepper, allspices, sugar, paprika, and oil. Stir and add salt to taste.

Cover the earthen pot and (if possible) seal with dough.

Bake at 700F for about 2 hours.

Serve with potato puree.

STUFFED RABBIT

Ingredients:

1 ½ lbs rabbit
1/3 lb rabbit's offal
1/3 lb mushrooms, chopped
1/3 lb rice
1/3 lb sunflower oil
1/3 lb red wine
1 onion, finely chopped
3 bay leaves
1 teaspoon savory
1 teaspoon ground black pepper
salt to taste
parsley

How to prepare:

In a saucepan, not too deep, fry the rabbit's offal in oil until soft.

Add the mushrooms, onion, black pepper, salt, parsley and rice and pour 2/3 lb water. Simmer until the water evaporates.

Stuff the rabbit with the mixture. Place it in a baking dish, pour the wine and the oil over it, sprinkle with paprika and salt, add ½ lb water in the baking dish, add the bay leaves and cover the dish with aluminum foil.

Bake 1 ½ hours at 540F. (If the rabbit is old, the time should be increased). 10 minutes before the end, uncover the rabbit and bake directly.

Note: You may add chopped potatoes and rice with vegetables in the baking dish. Thus you won't need to prepare side dishes.

CHICKEN KAVARMA

Ingredients:

2 lbs chicken meat
½ lb butter
2 lbs onion
2 lbs tomatoes
½ lb pepper
1 bunch of parsley, finely chopped
ground black pepper (optional)
salt to taste
sunflower oil

How to prepare:

Cut the meat in portions. Remove the bones. Salt the pieces of chicken meat according to your taste.

In a frying pan full of oil, fry the pieces for 5-10 minutes.

Peel the onion. Then chop it finely. Wash the tomatoes, peel and chop finely. Do the same with the peppers.

In another pan full of oil, place the ingredients in the following way: the onions, the peppers and the tomatoes.

Fry for 10 minutes and add the chicken meat. If necessary, add some water. Simmer until mild. Add the black pepper though you needn't if you don't like black pepper. But with it the dish is much more delicious.

Bake the dish into the oven for 20 minutes and, 5 minutes before the end, sprinkle with parsley.

Enjoy the dish with beer or white wine.

CHICKEN STEW

Ingredients:

1 ½ lb chicken meat, chopped
1 ½ lb potatoes, cubed
½ lb tomato puree
800 ml water
3 tablespoons sunflower oil
3 onions, finely chopped
1 red pepper, chopped
1 green pepper, chopped
1 teaspoon ground black pepper
1 teaspoon paprika
1 teaspoon savory
1 teaspoon salt
1 teaspoon all-purpose flour
parsley (optional)

How to prepare:

In a saucepan, fry the onion in the oil and peppers until soft.

When soft, add chicken and fry until it changes color. When ready, add the water, tomato puree, potatoes and the spices.

Simmer until the meat and potatoes are fully cooked.

Add 1 tablespoon ware to the flour and mix well. Add to the stew and simmer until it thickens.

Sprinkle with parsley (only if you like).

Serve hot.

WITHOUT MEAT

LENTIL STEW

This goes well with any sausages you may have. Serve separately or add the sausages, fried, to the lentils in the last minutes of How to prepare.

Ingredients:

1 cup lentils

1 onion, finely chopped

2 medium carrots, finely chopped

2 garlic cloves, chopped

2 tablespoons sunflower oil

1 can tomatoes, diced or 2 fresh tomatoes, peeled and diced

1 tablespoon savory or oregano

salt & pepper to taste

1 tablespoon corn flour or flour mixed with a little water

2 celery stalks, cut into small pieces (optional)

How to prepare:

Boil the lentils in slightly salted water for about 20 – 25 minutes. Heat the oil in a pan, sauté the onions, carrots and celery for about 5 minutes and simmer for about 10 minutes. Add the lentils, cooked and drained, the tomatoes and the garlic into the pan and simmer for another 10 – 15 minutes. Add the corn flour to thicken the dish, season with salt, pepper and savory.

PANAGYURSKI EGGS

This dish is named after Panagyurishte, small town full of history.

Ingredients:

3 eggs
1 cup strained yoghurt (or more, if you like)
1 teaspoon oil
a pinch of paprika
salt to taste
2 tablespoons vinegar
1 clove of garlic, crushed (optional)
2 cups water
parsley (optional)

How to prepare:

Add the vinegar and a pinch of salt to the boiling water. Break the eggs directly into the water. Boil for 3 to 5 minutes, depending on how runny you like your eggs.

Mix the yoghurt and the garlic, add very little salt. Put the eggs on top of that mixture.

Heat the oil and add paprika very careful not to burn it. It takes 10 seconds or less to burn. Immediately pour the curried oil over the eggs and yoghurt mixture and serve.

MISH – MASH (EGGS, PEPPERS, CHEESE)

Literally translated, mish-mash means "hodge-podge". This is a very tasty meal and it takes only 10 minutes to prepare. In the summertime, I prepare it when I don't have for more elaborate dishes.

Ingredients:

3 tomatoes, chopped
3 red peppers, chopped
1 onion, chopped
2 tablespoons vegetable oil
½ lb feta cheese, crumbled
3 eggs, beaten
some parsley (to your taste), chopped
salt and pepper to taste

How to prepare:

Heat the oil in a frying pan, add the onions and the peppers and cook until the onions are golden. Add the tomatoes and cook for another 3 minutes. Add the cheese and the eggs and cook for another 2-3 minutes. Sprinkle with parsley and serve hot or cold. Delicious with toast.

Note: If you have more time, you can roast the peppers. It is even more delicious that way.

CHEESE STUFFED PEPPERS

Ingredients:

6 medium green or red peppers (or both)
2 eggs
½ cup flour (or bread crumbs)
1/3 lb feta cheese, crumbled
¼ cup vegetable oil
1 tomato, chopped

How to prepare:

Bake, peel and seed the peppers. Beat an egg into a homogenous mixture.

Beat the other egg and mix it with the cheese, add the tomato and mix well. Stuff the peppers with the mixture; roll in flour or bread crumbs, then in the beaten egg, then again in flour.

Fry in the oil for about 3-4 minutes each side, turning only once. Serve hot or cold.

CHEESE SHOPSKI STYLE

Ingredients:

1 lb feta cheese
1/3 lb mozzarella
2 eggs
2 chilies
2 tomatoes, sliced
2 roasted pepper, chopped
a pinch of oregano
parsley

How to prepare:

Take two small pottery pots (in the picture) and put in each a layer of cheese, then a layer of peppers and tomatoes, then more cheese. Close the pots with the lids and bake for 20 minutes at 375F or until the cheese on top is melted.

Break an egg on top of each dish and bake for another 5 minutes.

FRIED COURGETTES

This is a very popular dish in Bulgaria and it can be a side dish as well as a starter. It is often prepared few hours in advance and left in the fridge to cool.

Ingredients:

4 courgettes, medium size, thinly sliced on diagonal
500 ml strained yoghurt
a bunch of fresh dill, finely chopped
2 cloves of garlic, pressed
1 cup all purpose flour
salt to taste

How to prepare:

Mix the garlic and chopped dill with 1 teaspoon salt in a small bowl. Mix in yoghurt.

Pour little oil into a heavy saucepan and heat to 350F. Place the flour into a medium bowl. Working in batches, pat dry the zucchini slices, add to the flour in the bowl and toss, separating slices to coat well.

Fry in small batches until golden, about 2-3 minutes per side. Transfer to paper towels and pat dry.

Place yoghurt in the centre of a large platter and surround with zucchini or just pour it over the courgettes as in the picture. Serve hot or cold.

POTATOES AU GRATIN

Ingredients:

2 lbs potatoes, chopped in cubes or sliced in discs
2 tablespoons butter
2 tablespoons flour
2 cups milk
1 tablespoon vegetable soup cubes
a pinch of black pepper
½ lb cheese (Swiss or mozzarella)
2 tablespoons fresh parsley
dill & mint, finely chopped

How to prepare:

Cook the potatoes in a cup of water until tender – about 20 minutes at 375F – in a covered pot. You can also boil or steam them, or cook them in the microwave.

Make the cheese béchamel sauce: fry the flour in the butter for 3 minutes, add the milk and stir until a smooth sauce forms. Add the cheese and stir until it completely melts.

Add the béchamel sauce to the potatoes and mix well=

Cook in the oven for 5–10 minutes. You may top with grated cheese and bake it in a open pan until a golden crust forms.

IMAMBAIALDA (STUFFED EGGPLANTS)

The recipe is actually Turkish but it has been deeply rooted in Bulgarian national cuisine ever since the years of the Ottoman Yoke. According to the legend, when the Turkish Imam (a ruler of a province) stopped at a small roadside pub, he asked for a plate of this favourite food of his, called something else at the time. It was prepared so well by the cook that the Imam asked for another one, and another one, and several more after that. He ate so much that in the end he couldn't move but could only say: *Imam bayalda*, meaning *"the Imam feels sick"*.

Ingredients:

4 eggplants
6 tomatoes, grated
5 onions, chopped
2 carrots, grated
1 celery, grated
4 cloves of garlic, finely chopped
half a lemon
1 bay leaf
parsley
peppers
½ cup sunflower oil
salt to taste

How to prepare:

Remove the top of the eggplants and scoop out the soft insides (you should end up having 4 hollow eggplants with half of their meat still on the sides).

Heat the oil and cook the onions until they become golden. Add the carrots, celery, tomatoes, garlic and parsley. Add the bay leaves and some water and sauté for 5 minutes.

Stuff the eggplants with the mixture (you can add some of their meat you scooped out if you don't have enough mixture to fill them with), top with a slice of tomato and bake for 25 minutes at 375F. Serve warm or cold.

EGGPLANTS IN TOMATO SAUCE

Ingredients:

2 medium eggplants, sliced in thin discs
1 cup oil
1 cup flour
1 can of chopped tomatoes
2 garlic cloves, crushed
a bunch of parsley, chopped
salt to taste
black pepper, crushed

How to prepare:

Season the eggplants with salt and leave aside for 10 minutes; then discard of the drained water. Dip each slice into the flour and fry in the 1/3 of the oil. You can also grill instead if you prefer using less oil in your diet. Let the slices cool. Heat the remaining oil in a pan; add half of the garlic and the tomatoes; stir and simmer for 3 minutes. Let it cool.

Make layers of tomato sauce and eggplants, finishing with tomato sauce. Sprinkle with parsley and serve.

RICE, SPINACH AND MUSHROOMS WITH YOGHURT SAUCE

Closely resembling risotto or pilaf, this traditional Bulgarian recipe for cooking rice is a delicious meal that can be served also as a side dish with roast or grilled lamb or even pork.

Ingredients:

1 lb fresh spinach, finely chopped
1 large onion, diced
½ lb fresh mushrooms, sliced
1 carrot, sliced
½ cup rice
4 spring onions, finely chopped
500 ml vegetable bouillon
1/3 cup olive oil
salt to taste
ground pepper to taste
parsley, finely chopped

For the yoghurt sauce:
2 cups yoghurt
a large garlic clove, grated or minced
salt to taste

How to prepare:

Heat the olive oil in a large skillet. Add the onion, carrot and mushrooms and cook until the carrot is soft.
While they are cooking, rinse the rice and drain. Add the rice to the skillet and cook for 2 minutes, stirring often. Start adding the vegetable bouillon in portions,

stirring and adding bouillon as the rice absorbs it. Cover and simmer.

Cook about 10 more minutes until all the liquid is absorbed and the rice is cooked (it may be necessary to add some water). Add the spinach, cover and cook until the spinach is cooked.

Remove from heat, mix well and season to taste.

How to prepare the sauce:

Mix the ingredients in a small bowl and stir gently to blend. Pour the sauce over the risotto, sprinkle with parsley and serve.

TOMATOES WITH RICE

An old and yet tasty Bulgarian dish. I cook it every time when I have no a better idea.

Ingredients:

1 large onion, chopped
1 cup rice
5-6 tomatoes, peeled and grated, or a can of tomato paste
1 teaspoon paprika
salt to taste
parsley
2-3 tablespoons sunflower oil
olives

How to prepare:

In a saucepan, fry the onion in the oil until soft. Add the rice and fry for another 5-6 minutes. Add the paprika, stir. Add the tomatoes. Simmer for 5 minutes. Add water – 4 cups. Simmer for 20 minutes or until the rice is fully cooked. Add salt and parsley and stir.

Serve warm or cold, garnished with olives.

GYUVETCH WITHOUT MEAT

Ingredients:

2 lbs potatoes, diced
1 vegetable marrow, diced
1-2 spring onions, chopped
½ lb French beans
2 tomatoes, peeled and finely chopped
½ lb okra
1 tablespoon parsley, chopped
1 tablespoon dill, chopped
¼ lb tomato paste
1 teaspoon paprika
salt to taste
olive oil to taste

How to prepare:

Mix the potatoes and the vegetable marrow. Add the onions, beans, tomatoes and okra. Add parsley and dill, salt, olive oil, paprika and tomato paste. Mix well, put in a baking dish or a clay pot and cover (almost) with water.

Preheat oven to 375F. Bake for an hour or until the vegetables are cooked. The water should evaporate completely.

PEAS WITH POTATOES

Ingredients:

1 lb peas
2 large potatoes, cubed
2 large carrots, chopped
1 red pepper, chopped
1 green pepper, chopped
1 clove of garlic, chopped
3 tablespoons sunflower oil
1 tablespoon paprika
½ bunch of parsley
1 large tomato, chopped
yoghurt

How to prepare:

Boil the peas, potatoes and carrots until ready.

In a deep pan, fry the peppers and garlic. Add the potatoes and carrots. Stew for a while (5-10 minutes).

Add the peas, tomato, paprika and salt. Sprinkle with parsley.

Serve with yoghurt.

PASTRIES AND PIES

PATATNIK (POTATO DISH)

You can prepare *patatnik* as a main course or a side dish. In the old times, during the cold winter months, potatoes used to be one of the main foods for all Bulgarians. They have even been used to make bread.

Ingredients:

6 tablespoons flour
½ cup vegetable oil
water

For the filling:
1 tablespoon butter, melted
3 lbs (around 10 big ones) potatoes, grated
4 onions, grated
3 eggs, beaten
1 teaspoon of fresh mint or dried oregano
½ tablespoon vegetable oil
½ teaspoon salt

How to prepare:

Make a soft paste of the flour, the oil and as much water as necessary. Leave it for 15 minutes on room temperature; then divide into 2 parts, one of them a little larger than the other. Spread the smaller part to form a sheet 4-5 cm larger than the bottom of your baking dish.

Mix together the potatoes, the onions, the eggs, the mint and the salt.

Place the bigger part of the paste in a buttered baking dish – it must cover the baking dish and stick out at all ends. Spread the filling on top and cover with the smaller sheet which you must have already prepared. Turn inside the ends of the first sheet and pinch the two sheets together to prevent the filling from coming out. Bake at 375F for about 25 minutes or until it turns rosy.

BANITSA

This is a traditional and very tasty Bulgarian pastry. There are a lot of different recipes, all of them equally tasty.

Ingredients:

1 pack of filo dough
3 eggs
1 lb Bulgarian cheese (or feta cheese)
3 tablespoons butter
1 cup of milk or yoghurt

How to prepare:

Mix the crumbled cheese, milk and eggs together. Don't over mix – cheese should be lumpy. Melt the butter in a cup. Butter the bottom of a casserole pan. Lay 5-6 sheets of filo dough, one after another (not together) as you spread some butter in between. Spread some of the cheese mixture on top; lay another 3-4 sheets, spreading butter in between. Repeat until all mixture is used. Lay the last 3-4 sheets on top with no butter in between. Spread the rest of the butter on top. Cut in portion sized squares and bake in the oven until golden (about 30 minutes on 400 F).

SPINACH BANITSA

Ingredients:

2 lbs flour
3 cups water

2 lbs spinach, finely chopped
1 lb feta cheese
1 ½ cups yoghurt (or milk)
4 tablespoons butter
1 tablespoon vegetable oil
1 teaspoon vinegar
a pinch of salt

How to prepare:

Cook the spinach in 1 tablespoon melted butter for 5 minutes. Let it cool and add it to the yoghurt and crumbled cheese mixture.

In another bowl, mix the flour, oil, vinegar, salt and water and knead until you get hard dough. Divide into 10 and roll into thin sheets. You can also use filo dough sheets from the store instead.

Spread some butter on the bottom of a baking dish, spread a sheet and top with the spinach feeling. Repeat until all sheets are done. Bake for about 35 minutes at 375 F.

MILK BANITSA

Ingredients:

2 lbs flour
9 eggs
2 cups milk
1 cup sugar
½ cup semolina
1 tablespoon vegetable oil
1 tablespoon vinegar
1 cup water

a pinch of salt
2 tablespoons butter

How to prepare:

Mix the flour, salt, 1 egg, vinegar and 3 cups water and knead not so hard dough. Roll into thin sheets (makes about 10). You can also use filo dough sheets from the store instead.

Place all sheets on a tray, one after another, basting each one with melted butter. Cut into squares or diamonds.

Bring the milk to the boiling point, add the sugar, the rest of the butter and semolina, constantly stirring. Leave to cool. Then add the 8 beaten eggs. Mix well and pour over the pastry sheets.

Bake for about 25 minutes at 375F.

Sprinkle with powdered sugar and serve.

RHODOPEAN PIE

Ingredients:

For the dough:
1 tablespoon vinegar
1 tablespoon oil
1/3 lb water
flour

For the filling:
½ lb butter
5 eggs, beaten
cheese
cooked rice

How to prepare:

Knead the dough. Roll the dough into 2 thin round flat pieces. Make the one smaller than the other.

Oil one round casserole pan.

Place the larger half of the though in the pan. (Some of the dough should overlap the pan by an inch all around.)

Mix all the ingredients for the filling.

Spread the filling over the dough. Pull excess dough over the top to enclose the filling.

Place the smaller half of the dough on top to enclose the filling completely.

Cook at a medium heat for 20 minutes, slowly adding small amounts of butter from the sides of the pie. Carefully flip over the pie and continue cooking for another 20 minutes, adding butter.

BANITSA WITH LEEKS AND CHEESE

Ingredients:

1 lb filo dough
4 eggs
2/3 lb cheese, crumbled
3 leeks, chopped in thin circles
2 tablespoons vegetable oil
1 teaspoon savory
salt to taste

How to prepare:

In a pan, fry the leeks until soft. Add salt and savory. Stir.

After it cools, add the cheese and 3 beaten eggs.

Oil the bottom of a baking dish. Spread a sheet of filo dough, then spread some of the filling. Then another sheet and some of the filling again. Repeat until you have spread all the sheets of filo dough. You should finish with a sheet.

Beat the last egg and spread over the last sheet.
Preheat oven to 400F. Bake until ready.

BANITSA WITH MEAT

Ingredients:

for the filling:

1 tablespoon olive oil
1 medium onion, chopped
2 cloves of garlic, minced
1 lb minced meat (beef, pork, veal or a combination)
½ cup parsley, finely chopped
1 ½ teaspoon salt
½ teaspoon ground black pepper
¼ teaspoon paprika

1 cup yoghurt
½ cup olive oil
1 egg
½ lb filo dough

How to prepare:

In a deep and a large pan, fry the onion in the oil, stirring often until soft (about 3 minutes). Add the garlic and fry for 30 seconds. Add the minced meat, stirring constantly, and fry until ready and changes color. Add the parsley, salt, black pepper and paprika. Fry for 2 minutes more, stirring constantly, then remove from the stove.

In a bowl, mix the yoghurt, the olive oil and the beaten egg. Spread a thin layer of the mixture on the bottom of a baking dish.

Preheat oven to 375F.

Place a sheet of filo dough over the spread mixture in the baking dish. Carefully spread some of the yoghurt and egg mixture. Repeat until you have placed half of the sheets of filo dough. Spread the filling. Place another sheet of filo dough and spread some of the yoghurt and egg mixture. Repeat until all the sheets are done, finishing with a mixture.

Bake for 40 minutes or until the dish is ready. Cool for ten minutes before serving.

BANITSA WITH SAUERKRAUT

Ingredients:

1 lb filo dough
2 lbs sauerkraut, chopped
2-3 leeks, finely chopped
salt to taste
1 cup oil for frying
1/3 cup vegetable oil
ground black pepper (optional)

How to prepare:

Fry the sauerkraut in ½ cup vegetable oil until soft.

In another pan, fry the leeks in ½ cup vegetable oil. Season with salt to taste and a little black pepper (optional).

In an oiled baking dish, place two sheets of filo dough. Sprinkle with vegetable oil, spread some of the sauerkraut filling, then some of the leeks filling. Then again 2 sheets of filo dough, sauerkraut, leeks, etc.

Finish with 2 sheets of filo dough. Cut the pie in squares, pour 1 cup of water over it and sprinkle with vegetable oil.

Bake at 375F until changes color or until ready.

MEKITSI (FRIED DOUGH PASTRY)

Ingredients:

2 lbs flour
3 eggs
1 lb yoghurt (you can use milk instead)
a pack of yeast (or 1 teaspoon of baking soda)
1 cup water
½ teaspoon salt
1 cup oil

How to prepare:

Add yeast to some lukewarm water and let it stay for 5 minutes to get bubbly.

Beat the eggs, mix with the yoghurt (milk) and water. Add flour and continue to mix until you get soft dough. Leave it for an hour.

Roll into a sheet and cut out circles (you can use a teacup). Fry in plenty of oil (deep fryer will do) until golden brown. Serve powdered with sugar. They go well with jam and feta cheese too.

BAKLAVA

We don't claim baklava is a Bulgarian dish. It is claimed by almost every Balkan state as its own invention. In some countries, it is known as a Greek pastry, although it is Turkish. There are almost as many recipes for *baklava* as for *banitsa*.

Ingredients:

1 pack of filo dough
1 lb walnuts, chopped
1 teaspoon vanilla (or use vanilla sugar)
4 tablespoons of butter, melted
4 ¼ cups sugar
2 cups water
1 teaspoon lemon juice

How to prepare:

Make the syrup first. Boil the water and sugar for about 15 minutes. Add lemon juice and boil another 10 minutes. Set aside to cool.

then make the filling: mix the walnuts, ¼ cup of sugar and vanilla. Take out a sheet of dough and place it in the baking pan. Brush the dough with melted butter. Repeat 10-12 times. Then repeat the same for the half of the sheets. Spread the walnut filling across the tray. Do the rest of the dough sheets in the same way as the first half. Cut into squares. Bake at 325F for about 60 minutes or until golden brown. Add the syrup.

Serve after 24 hours.

SARALIISKA BANITSA

Ingredients:

2 lbs flour
½ cup walnut kernels
4 cups sugar
6 cups water
vanilla
a pinch of salt
2 tablespoons butter

How to prepare:

Mix the flour, salt and 3 cups water and knead not so hard dough. Roll into thin sheets (makes about 10). You can also use filo dough sheets from the shop instead. Baste each sheet with butter and top with crushed walnut kernels.

Roll the sheets, arrange in a circle and bake for about 35 minutes at 375F. Leave to cool.

Boil the sugar and the vanilla with 3 cups of water.

After *banitsa* has cooled, pour over the hot syrup.

PUMPKIN BANITSA

Ingredients:

1-2 lbs pie pumpkin, peeled and seeded, or 1 lb can pumpkin puree

4 ounces (1 stick) butter plus 1 cup (2 sticks) melted butter

1 cup sugar

1 cup chopped walnuts

½ teaspoon cinnamon
16 sheets filo dough, thawed

How to prepare:

Grate the pumpkin. Melt 4 ounces butter in a large saucepan, add pumpkin and sugar, cooking until pumpkin is tender. Let cool and add walnuts and cinnamon.

If using canned pumpkin, transfer to a bowl and add sugar, walnuts and cinnamon, mixing well.

Preheat the oven to 750F. Fold one filo dough sheet in half so it measures 12 inches by 8 inches. Brush lightly with melted butter.

Portion out a ½ inch strip of feeling along either the 12-inch edge if you want an S-shaped scroll, or along the 8-inch edge for a cigar-shaped roll and ¼ inch away from the edges. Fold up bottom edge first, then sides and then roll away from yourself until you have a tight cylinder. Brush lightly with more melted butter.

Repeat with the remaining 15 sheets of filo dough. Shape the long cylinders into S shapes or leave the short cylinders as they are and place them in an oiled pan. Bake for 20 minutes or until golden brown and crispy.

Serve warm or cold.

Note: I sometimes prepare a syrup for baklava and pour over the pumpkin banitsa. It is more delicious that way but you can try both variants and decide for yourself.

Printed in Great Britain
by Amazon